MY PET PEEVES

KNOCK
KNOCK®
VENICE, CALIFORNIA

Created and published by Knock Knock
Distributed by Who's There Inc.
Venice, CA 90291
knockknockstuff.com

© 2013 Who's There Inc.
All rights reserved
Knock Knock is a trademark of Who's There Inc.
Made in China

ISBN: 978-160106448-6
UPC: 825703-50078-3

10 9 8 7 6 5 4 3 2

LIFE SURE CAN BE
ANNOYING

Whether it's all the little things (double-parking, dirty dishes, the smacking sound your partner makes when eating cereal) that inspire your ire or the big stuff (litterbugs, uncivil political debate, the continued popularity of reality television programming), there is a lot to be upset about. While the world would have you take deep breaths and passively accept these egregious grievances, most of us are incapable of just letting it go. And you're not alone—we're all a little peeved about something.

In fact, you're in great company. Famous—and infamous—grumblers are as numerous as the very things people tend to grumble about. This esteemed list includes everyone from television personalities such as Andy Rooney to comedians such as Larry David and George Carlin to writers Ambrose Bierce, Dorothy Parker, and Oscar Wilde. These celebrated curmudgeons help remind us that despite today's "I'm okay, you're okay" culture, sometimes a dose of brutal honesty offers the most relief. So, while you may not be able to change every driver's tailgating habit, you *can* perhaps change your mood by pinpointing what's currently got your goat.

And what better place to gain some perspective—without taking it out on the entire world—than on these very pages? A journal provides a private place to chronicle your indignation so you can get on with the good stuff. In addition to helping put one's mind at ease, journal writing has been shown to be good for your health. Proven benefits include better stress management, strengthened immune systems, fewer doctor visits, and improvement in chronic illnesses such as asthma. "It's hard to believe," says James W. Pennebaker, a psychology professor at the University of Texas at Austin, but "being able to put experiences into words is good for your physical health."

It's not entirely clear how journaling accomplishes all this. Catharsis is involved, but many also point to the value of organizing experiences into a coherent narrative. According to *Newsweek*, some experts believe that journaling "forces us to transform the ruminations cluttering our minds into coherent stories." Writing about an experience can help solidify what you have to feel hopeful about. In many ways, journaling can help us to see the larger picture and get past the small stuff (which can seem so big).

Specialists agree that in order to reap the benefits of journaling you have to stick with it, quasi-daily, for as little as five minutes at a time (at least fifteen minutes, however, is best), even on the days you can't find a single thing to complain about. Finding regular writing times and comfortable locations can help with consistency. If you find yourself unable to muster a single pet peeve, don't stress. Instead, use the quotes inside this journal as a jumping-off point for observations and explorations. Renowned journaler Anaïs Nin suggests asking yourself, "What feels vivid, warm, or near to you at the moment?" Write whatever comes to you, and don't criticize it; journaling is a process of self-reflection, not a structured composition. In other words, spew. Finally, determine a home for your journal where you can reference it whenever and wherever you're feeling vexed.

As the great William Shakespeare famously proclaimed, "Life is as tedious as a twice-told tale." Take it from the man who had the patience to write close to forty epic plays without a word processor: life is worth grousing about. Before you know it, your list of pet peeves will dwindle, and you might even start to enjoy humanity a little—or even a lot—more on a daily basis. Now go forth and find something to gripe about!

I don't have pet peeves, I have whole kennels of irritation.

Whoopi Goldberg

WHY I'M PEEVED TODAY:

_____

_____

_____

_____

_____

_____

_____

_____

_____

_____

_____

_____

_____

_____

_____

_____

_____

_____

_____

_____

HOW TO LET OFF STEAM TODAY:

My loathings are simple: stupidity, oppression, crime, cruelty, soft music.

Vladimir Nabokov

WHY I'M PEEVED TODAY:

_____

_____

_____

_____

_____

_____

_____

_____

_____

_____

_____

_____

_____

_____

_____

_____

_____

HOW TO LET OFF STEAM TODAY:

What a blessing it would be if we could open and shut our ears as easily as we do our eyes.

Georg Christoph Lichtenberg

WHY I'M PEEVED TODAY:

_____

_____

_____

_____

_____

_____

_____

_____

_____

_____

_____

_____

_____

_____

_____

_____

_____

_____

_____

HOW TO LET OFF STEAM TODAY:

I prefer a convenient vice to a fatiguing virtue.

Molière

DATE

WHY I'M PEEVED TODAY:

_____

_____

_____

_____

_____

_____

_____

_____

_____

_____

_____

_____

_____

_____

_____

HOW TO LET OFF STEAM TODAY:

Charming villains have always had a decided social advantage over well-meaning people who chew with their mouths open.

Judith Martin

WHY I'M PEEVED TODAY:

HOW TO LET OFF STEAM TODAY:

I assure you that the typewriting machine, when played with expression, is not more annoying than the piano when played by a sister or near relation.

Oscar Wilde

WHY I'M PEEVED TODAY:

_____

_____

_____

_____

_____

_____

_____

_____

_____

_____

_____

_____

_____

_____

_____

_____

HOW TO LET OFF STEAM TODAY:

I go from exasperation to a state of collapse, then I recover and go from prostration to fury, so that my average state is one of being annoyed.

Gustave Flaubert

DATE

WHY I'M PEEVED TODAY:

_____

_____

_____

_____

_____

_____

_____

_____

_____

_____

_____

_____

_____

_____

_____

_____

_____

_____

HOW TO LET OFF STEAM TODAY:

It is better to have
a relationship with
someone who cheats
on you than with
someone who does
not flush the toilet.

Uma Thurman

DATE		

WHY I'M PEEVED TODAY:

_____

_____

_____

_____

_____

_____

_____

_____

_____

_____

_____

_____

_____

_____

_____

_____

_____

_____

_____

HOW TO LET OFF STEAM TODAY:

Ignorant people think it's the noise which fighting cats make that is so aggravating, but it ain't so; it's the sickening grammar they use.

Mark Twain

WHY I'M PEEVED TODAY:

_____

_____

_____

_____

_____

_____

_____

_____

_____

_____

_____

_____

_____

_____

_____

_____

_____

_____

HOW TO LET OFF STEAM TODAY:

Aw, how's that for disgusting?
If I watch any more of this hugging,
I'm gonna get sick to my stomach!
Let's get out of here!

Oscar the Grouch

WHY I'M PEEVED TODAY:

_____

_____

_____

_____

_____

_____

_____

_____

_____

_____

_____

_____

_____

_____

_____

_____

_____

_____

_____

HOW TO LET OFF STEAM TODAY:

I don't dislike babies,
though I think very
young ones rather
disgusting.

Queen Victoria

DATE

WHY I'M PEEVED TODAY:

HOW TO LET OFF STEAM TODAY:

When I was young, I found out
that the big toe always ends up
making a hole in a sock.
So I stopped wearing socks.

Albert Einstein

DATE

WHY I'M PEEVED TODAY:

_____

_____

_____

_____

_____

_____

_____

_____

_____

_____

_____

_____

_____

_____

_____

_____

_____

_____

_____

_____

HOW TO LET OFF STEAM TODAY:

Arriving late was a way of saying that your own time was more valuable than the time of the person who waited for you.

Karen Joy Fowler

DATE

WHY I'M PEEVED TODAY:

_____

_____

_____

_____

_____

_____

_____

_____

_____

_____

_____

_____

_____

_____

_____

_____

HOW TO LET OFF STEAM TODAY:

To have a
grievance
is to have
a purpose
in life.

Eric Hoffer

DATE

WHY I'M PEEVED TODAY:

HOW TO LET OFF STEAM TODAY:

A hat should be taken off when you greet a lady and left off for the rest of your life. Nothing looks more stupid than a hat.

P. J. O'Rourke

DATE		

WHY I'M PEEVED TODAY:

_____

_____

_____

_____

_____

_____

_____

_____

_____

_____

_____

_____

_____

_____

_____

_____

_____

_____

_____

_____

_____

HOW TO LET OFF STEAM TODAY:

Your next-door neighbor is not a man; he is an environment. He is the barking of a dog, he is the noise of a piano; he is a dispute about a wall; he is drains that are worse than yours, or roses that are better than yours.

G. K. Chesterton

WHY I'M PEEVED TODAY:

HOW TO LET OFF STEAM TODAY:

I can't stand a naked light bulb, any more than I can stand a rude remark or a vulgar action.

Tennessee Williams

WHY I'M PEEVED TODAY:

_____

_____

_____

_____

_____

_____

_____

_____

_____

_____

_____

_____

_____

_____

_____

_____

_____

HOW TO LET OFF STEAM TODAY:

A person who is nice to you, but rude to the waiter, is not a nice person.

Dave Barry

DATE

WHY I'M PEEVED TODAY:

_____

_____

_____

_____

_____

_____

_____

_____

_____

_____

_____

_____

_____

_____

_____

_____

_____

HOW TO LET OFF STEAM TODAY:

If you are a dog and your owner suggests that you wear a sweater ... suggest that he wear a tail.

Fran Lebowitz

DATE

WHY I'M PEEVED TODAY:

_____

_____

_____

_____

_____

_____

_____

_____

_____

_____

_____

_____

_____

_____

_____

_____

HOW TO LET OFF STEAM TODAY:

I don't answer the phone. I get the feeling whenever I do that there will be someone on the other end.

Fred Couples

WHY I'M PEEVED TODAY:

HOW TO LET OFF STEAM TODAY:

In my mind, there is nothing so illiberal, and so ill-bred, as audible laughter.

Lord Chesterfield

WHY I'M PEEVED TODAY:

_____

_____

_____

_____

_____

_____

_____

_____

_____

_____

_____

_____

_____

_____

_____

_____

_____

_____

HOW TO LET OFF STEAM TODAY:

There cannot be a greater rudeness, than to interrupt another in the current of his discourse.

John Locke

WHY I'M PEEVED TODAY:

_____

_____

_____

_____

_____

_____

_____

_____

_____

_____

_____

_____

_____

_____

_____

_____

HOW TO LET OFF STEAM TODAY:

I personally think we developed language because of our deep need to complain.

Lily Tomlin

DATE

WHY I'M PEEVED TODAY:

_____

_____

_____

_____

_____

_____

_____

_____

_____

_____

_____

_____

_____

_____

_____

_____

_____

HOW TO LET OFF STEAM TODAY:

I really hate people who go on an airplane in jogging outfits ... You see eighty-year-old women coming on the plane in jogging outfits for comfort. Well, my comfort—my mental comfort—is completely ruined when I see them coming.

John Waters

WHY I'M PEEVED TODAY:

HOW TO LET OFF STEAM TODAY:

Better never than late.

George Bernard Shaw

WHY I'M PEEVED TODAY:

HOW TO LET OFF STEAM TODAY:

We are the Few, the Proud, the Appalled at Everyone Else.

David Foster Wallace

DATE

WHY I'M PEEVED TODAY:

_____

_____

_____

_____

_____

_____

_____

_____

_____

_____

_____

_____

_____

_____

_____

_____

_____

HOW TO LET OFF STEAM TODAY:

Are you happy with that park? You're way outside the line; you're taking up two spaces ... That's just shoddy. It's not an open field. It's not a farm. Just park your car between the lines. It's not that hard. Just pull in between the lines.

Larry David

WHY I'M PEEVED TODAY:

_____

_____

_____

_____

_____

_____

_____

_____

_____

_____

_____

_____

_____

_____

_____

_____

HOW TO LET OFF STEAM TODAY:

If it keeps up, man will atrophy all his limbs but the push-button finger.

Frank Lloyd Wright

WHY I'M PEEVED TODAY:

_____

_____

_____

_____

_____

_____

_____

_____

_____

_____

_____

_____

_____

_____

_____

_____

_____

_____

HOW TO LET OFF STEAM TODAY:

A grouch escapes
so many little
annoyances that it
almost pays to be one.

Kin Hubbard

WHY I'M PEEVED TODAY:

HOW TO LET OFF STEAM TODAY:

My pet peeve is when someone next to you has something in their hair, and you want to pick it out, but they're strangers and you don't want to touch them.

Omar Epps

WHY I'M PEEVED TODAY:

_____

_____

_____

_____

_____

_____

_____

_____

_____

_____

_____

_____

_____

_____

_____

_____

_____

_____

HOW TO LET OFF STEAM TODAY:

Life is as tedious as a twice-told tale.

William Shakespeare

WHY I'M PEEVED TODAY:

_____

_____

_____

_____

_____

_____

_____

_____

_____

_____

_____

_____

_____

_____

_____

_____

_____

HOW TO LET OFF STEAM TODAY:

There is always one dude in front of you who takes 45 minutes at the car-rental counter. I don't know if this guy just pulled out trading stamps or his merchant marine ID or what.
But I am always behind him.

Adam Carolla

DATE

WHY I'M PEEVED TODAY:

_____

_____

_____

_____

_____

_____

_____

_____

_____

_____

_____

_____

_____

_____

_____

_____

_____

HOW TO LET OFF STEAM TODAY:

Between friends differences in taste or opinion are irritating in direct proportion to their triviality.

W. H. Auden

DATE

WHY I'M PEEVED TODAY:

_____

_____

_____

_____

_____

_____

_____

_____

_____

_____

_____

_____

_____

_____

_____

_____

_____

HOW TO LET OFF STEAM TODAY:

When I hear people say "oversimplistic," I suspect they don't know that "simplistic" means that all by itself. I wish somebody would drive "arguably" and "quite possibly" into the sea. And it seems to me it's almost always a bad idea to begin a sentence with "I pride myself on."

Geoff Nunberg

WHY I'M PEEVED TODAY:

_____

_____

_____

_____

_____

_____

_____

_____

_____

_____

_____

_____

_____

_____

_____

_____

_____

HOW TO LET OFF STEAM TODAY:

If I see someone's clothing tag hanging out, I freak out. Even if I don't know the person, I'll go up and fix it.

Kelly Clarkson

DATE

WHY I'M PEEVED TODAY:

_____

_____

_____

_____

_____

_____

_____

_____

_____

_____

_____

_____

_____

_____

_____

_____

_____

_____

_____

HOW TO LET OFF STEAM TODAY:

Have you ever noticed that anyone driving slower than you is an idiot, and anyone going faster is a maniac?

George Carlin

WHY I'M PEEVED TODAY:

_____

_____

_____

_____

_____

_____

_____

_____

_____

_____

_____

_____

_____

_____

_____

_____

HOW TO LET OFF STEAM TODAY:

I can't complain, but sometimes I still do.

Joe Walsh

DATE

WHY I'M PEEVED TODAY:

_____

_____

_____

_____

_____

_____

_____

_____

_____

_____

_____

_____

_____

_____

_____

_____

_____

HOW TO LET OFF STEAM TODAY:

I hate chewing gum ... When people chew loudly or smack it and pull it out of their mouth, that's the worst.

Oprah Winfrey

DATE

WHY I'M PEEVED TODAY:

_____

_____

_____

_____

_____

_____

_____

_____

_____

_____

_____

_____

_____

_____

_____

_____

HOW TO LET OFF STEAM TODAY:

ACCORDION, n. An instrument in harmony with the sentiments of an assassin.

Ambrose Bierce

DATE

WHY I'M PEEVED TODAY:

_____

_____

_____

_____

_____

_____

_____

_____

_____

_____

_____

_____

_____

_____

_____

_____

HOW TO LET OFF STEAM TODAY:

When I said I didn't have a cent, I didn't. I used to get annoyed with people who said they were broke when they had five dollars.

Paul Lynde

WHY I'M PEEVED TODAY:

_____

_____

_____

_____

_____

_____

_____

_____

_____

_____

_____

_____

_____

_____

_____

_____

HOW TO LET OFF STEAM TODAY:

There is no more miserable human being than one in whom nothing is habitual but indecision.

William James

DATE

WHY I'M PEEVED TODAY:

_____

_____

_____

_____

_____

_____

_____

_____

_____

_____

_____

_____

_____

_____

_____

_____

_____

HOW TO LET OFF STEAM TODAY:

Every year, back Spring comes,
with the nasty little birds yapping
their fool heads off, and the ground
all mucked up with arbutus.

Dorothy Parker

DATE

WHY I'M PEEVED TODAY:

_____

_____

_____

_____

_____

_____

_____

_____

_____

_____

_____

_____

_____

_____

_____

_____

_____

HOW TO LET OFF STEAM TODAY:

You go to the beach and you see people just lying there. Read a book! Read a magazine! Go swimming! What are you, a plant?

Ian Shoales

DATE

WHY I'M PEEVED TODAY:

_____

_____

_____

_____

_____

_____

_____

_____

_____

_____

_____

_____

_____

_____

_____

_____

_____

HOW TO LET OFF STEAM TODAY:

I love mankind— it's people I can't stand!

Charles M. Schulz

DATE

WHY I'M PEEVED TODAY:

_____
_____
_____
_____
_____
_____
_____
_____
_____
_____
_____
_____
_____
_____
_____
_____
_____
_____
_____

HOW TO LET OFF STEAM TODAY:

If writers wrote
as carelessly as
some people talk,
then adhasdh
asdglaseuyt[bn[
pasdlgkhasdfasdf.

Lemony Snicket

WHY I'M PEEVED TODAY:

_____

_____

_____

_____

_____

_____

_____

_____

_____

_____

_____

_____

_____

_____

_____

_____

_____

HOW TO LET OFF STEAM TODAY:

There is nobody so
irritating as somebody
with less intelligence
and more sense than
we have.

Don Herold

DATE

WHY I'M PEEVED TODAY:

_____

_____

_____

_____

_____

_____

_____

_____

_____

_____

_____

_____

_____

_____

_____

_____

HOW TO LET OFF STEAM TODAY:

I hate being high-fived. Do I look like the kind of girl that likes to be high-fived?

Dita Von Teese

WHY I'M PEEVED TODAY:

_____

_____

_____

_____

_____

_____

_____

_____

_____

_____

_____

_____

_____

_____

_____

_____

_____

HOW TO LET OFF STEAM TODAY:

Hanging is too good for
a man who makes puns;
he should be drawn and quoted.

Fred Allen

WHY I'M PEEVED TODAY:

_____

_____

_____

_____

_____

_____

_____

_____

_____

_____

_____

_____

_____

_____

_____

_____

_____

HOW TO LET OFF STEAM TODAY:

Shut your traps and stop kicking the seats! We're trying to watch the movie. And if I have to tell you again, we're gonna take it outside and I'm gonna show you what it's like!

George Costanza (*Seinfeld*)

WHY I'M PEEVED TODAY:

_____

_____

_____

_____

_____

_____

_____

_____

_____

_____

_____

_____

_____

_____

_____

_____

_____

_____

HOW TO LET OFF STEAM TODAY:

Outside of traffic, there is nothing that has held this country back as much as committees.

Will Rogers

WHY I'M PEEVED TODAY:

Why don't you get a haircut? You look like a chrysanthemum.

P. G. Wodehouse

DATE

WHY I'M PEEVED TODAY:

_____

_____

_____

_____

_____

_____

_____

_____

_____

_____

_____

_____

_____

_____

_____

_____

_____

HOW TO LET OFF STEAM TODAY:

No man lives without jostling and being jostled; in all ways he has to elbow himself through the world, giving and receiving offence.

Thomas Carlyle

DATE

WHY I'M PEEVED TODAY:

_____

_____

_____

_____

_____

_____

_____

_____

_____

_____

_____

_____

_____

_____

_____

_____

_____

HOW TO LET OFF STEAM TODAY:

Oh, the noise!
Oh, the Noise!
Noise! Noise! Noise!

Dr. Seuss

DATE

WHY I'M PEEVED TODAY:

_____

_____

_____

_____

_____

_____

_____

_____

_____

_____

_____

_____

_____

_____

_____

_____

_____

_____

HOW TO LET OFF STEAM TODAY:

I don't like food that's too carefully arranged ... If I wanted a picture I'd buy a painting.

Andy Rooney

DATE

WHY I'M PEEVED TODAY:

_____

_____

_____

_____

_____

_____

_____

_____

_____

_____

_____

_____

_____

_____

_____

_____

_____

_____

HOW TO LET OFF STEAM TODAY:

Of all the consumer products, chewing gum is perhaps the most ridiculous: it literally has no nourishment—you just chew it to give yourself something to do with your stupid idiot Western mouth.

Russell Brand

DATE

WHY I'M PEEVED TODAY:

_____
_____
_____
_____
_____
_____
_____
_____
_____
_____
_____
_____
_____
_____
_____
_____
_____
_____
_____

HOW TO LET OFF STEAM TODAY:

Those who do not complain are never pitied.

Jane Austen

WHY I'M PEEVED TODAY:

_____

_____

_____

_____

_____

_____

_____

_____

_____

_____

_____

_____

_____

_____

_____

_____

HOW TO LET OFF STEAM TODAY:

Oh the nerves, the nerves; the mysteries of this machine called Man! Oh, the little that unhinges it; poor creatures that we are!

Charles Dickens

DATE

WHY I'M PEEVED TODAY:

_____

_____

_____

_____

_____

_____

_____

_____

_____

_____

_____

_____

_____

_____

_____

_____

_____

_____

_____

_____

HOW TO LET OFF STEAM TODAY:

There's still the outside world to contend with, a world of backfiring cars and their human equivalents.

David Sedaris

WHY I'M PEEVED TODAY:

_____

_____

_____

_____

_____

_____

_____

_____

_____

_____

_____

_____

_____

_____

_____

_____

_____

_____

_____

HOW TO LET OFF STEAM TODAY:

He is simply a shiver looking for a spine to run up.

Paul Keating

DATE

WHY I'M PEEVED TODAY:

_____

_____

_____

_____

_____

_____

_____

_____

_____

_____

_____

_____

_____

_____

_____

_____

_____

_____

HOW TO LET OFF STEAM TODAY:

Golden Delicious apples. Where do they get off naming their apples that? That's a little immodest, isn't it? What if I called myself "Incredibly Attractive Ellen"?

Ellen DeGeneres

DATE

WHY I'M PEEVED TODAY:

_____

_____

_____

_____

_____

_____

_____

_____

_____

_____

_____

_____

_____

_____

_____

_____

_____

HOW TO LET OFF STEAM TODAY:

My second favorite household chore is ironing. My first being hitting my head on the top bunk bed until I faint.

Erma Bombeck

WHY I'M PEEVED TODAY:

_____

_____

_____

_____

_____

_____

_____

_____

_____

_____

_____

_____

_____

_____

_____

_____

_____

HOW TO LET OFF STEAM TODAY:

There is something about a home aquarium which sets my teeth on edge the moment I see it. Why anyone should want to live with a small container of stagnant water populated by a half-dead guppy is beyond me.

S. J. Perelman

WHY I'M PEEVED TODAY:

_____

_____

_____

_____

_____

_____

_____

_____

_____

_____

_____

_____

_____

_____

_____

_____

_____

HOW TO LET OFF STEAM TODAY:

I believe that treating other people well is a lost art.

Tim Gunn

WHY I'M PEEVED TODAY:

_____

_____

_____

_____

_____

_____

_____

_____

_____

_____

_____

_____

_____

_____

_____

_____

_____

_____

HOW TO LET OFF STEAM TODAY:

The words "pet" and "peeve."
Aren't they just irritating-sounding
in their own right? "Pet peeve"—
it makes my skin crawl.

Carson Kressley

WHY I'M PEEVED TODAY:

_____

_____

_____

_____

_____

_____

_____

_____

_____

_____

_____

_____

_____

_____

_____

_____

_____

_____

_____

HOW TO LET OFF STEAM TODAY:

I have noticed that the people who are late are often so much jollier than the people who have to wait for them.

E. V. Lucas

WHY I'M PEEVED TODAY:

_____

_____

_____

_____

_____

_____

_____

_____

_____

_____

_____

_____

_____

_____

_____

_____

_____

_____

HOW TO LET OFF STEAM TODAY:

The most common of all antagonisms arises from a man's taking a seat beside you on the train, a seat to which he is completely entitled.

Robert Benchley

| DATE |
| | | |

WHY I'M PEEVED TODAY:

_____

_____

_____

_____

_____

_____

_____

_____

_____

_____

_____

_____

_____

_____

_____

_____

_____

_____

HOW TO LET OFF STEAM TODAY:

The talk I hear among civilized people, which used to be fairly grammatical until about twelve or fifteen years ago, has now gone completely to pot.

John Simon

WHY I'M PEEVED TODAY:

HOW TO LET OFF STEAM TODAY:

Men who consistently leave the toilet seat up secretly want women to get up to go to the bathroom in the middle of the night and fall in.

Rita Rudner

WHY I'M PEEVED TODAY:

HOW TO LET OFF STEAM TODAY:

Some people can stay longer in an hour than others can in a week.

William Dean Howells

DATE

WHY I'M PEEVED TODAY:

_____

_____

_____

_____

_____

_____

_____

_____

_____

_____

_____

_____

_____

_____

_____

_____

_____

HOW TO LET OFF STEAM TODAY:

This strange beating together of hands has no meaning. To me it is very disturbing. We try to make sounds like music, and then in between comes this strange sound.

Leopold Stokowski

DATE

WHY I'M PEEVED TODAY:

_____

_____

_____

_____

_____

_____

_____

_____

_____

_____

_____

_____

_____

_____

_____

_____

_____

_____

HOW TO LET OFF STEAM TODAY:

Don't confuse being stimulating with being blunt.

Barbara Walters

WHY I'M PEEVED TODAY:

_____

_____

_____

_____

_____

_____

_____

_____

_____

_____

_____

_____

_____

_____

_____

_____

_____

_____

_____

_____

_____

HOW TO LET OFF STEAM TODAY:

And isn't your life extremely flat

With nothing whatever
    to grumble at!

W. S. Gilbert

DATE

WHY I'M PEEVED TODAY:

_____

_____

_____

_____

_____

_____

_____

_____

_____

_____

_____

_____

_____

_____

_____

_____

_____

HOW TO LET OFF STEAM TODAY:

I only go
out to get
me a fresh
appetite for
being alone.

Lord Byron

WHY I'M PEEVED TODAY:

_____

_____

_____

_____

_____

_____

_____

_____

_____

_____

_____

_____

_____

_____

_____

_____

_____

_____

HOW TO LET OFF STEAM TODAY:

The world is made up for the most part of morons and natural tyrants, sure of themselves, strong in their own opinions, never doubting anything.

Clarence Darrow

WHY I'M PEEVED TODAY:

_____

_____

_____

_____

_____

_____

_____

_____

_____

_____

_____

_____

_____

_____

_____

_____

HOW TO LET OFF STEAM TODAY:

If you have to dry the dishes
(Such an awful, boring chore)
If you have to dry the dishes
('Stead of going to the store)
If you have to dry the dishes
And you drop one on the floor—
Maybe they won't let you
Dry the dishes anymore.

Shel Silverstein

DATE

WHY I'M PEEVED TODAY:

_____

_____

_____

_____

_____

_____

_____

_____

_____

_____

_____

_____

_____

_____

_____

_____

HOW TO LET OFF STEAM TODAY:

I spit my last breath at thee.

Herman Melville

WHY I'M PEEVED TODAY:

_____

_____

_____

_____

_____

_____

_____

_____

_____

_____

_____

_____

_____

_____

_____

_____

_____

HOW TO LET OFF STEAM TODAY:

God knows I've got so many frailties myself, I ought to be able to understand and forgive them in others. But I don't.

Ava Gardner